Journey into Jazz

Columbus, OH

Front Cover, 3 © Bettmann / CORBIS; **6-7** © John Springer Collection / CORBIS; **8-12** © Bettmann / CORBIS; **15** © Bob Sacha / CORBIS; **Back Cover** © Bettmann / CORBIS.

SRAonline.com

An Open Court Curriculum.

Printed in China.

Send all inquiries to this address:
SRA/McGraw-Hill
4400 Easton Commons
Columbus, OH 43219

ISBN: 978-0-07-608858-4
MHID: 0-07-608858-8

1 2 3 4 5 6 7 8 9 NOR 13 12 11 10 09 08 07

The McGraw·Hill Companies

As night falls in New Orleans, Louisiana, musicians gather on a small stage in a club. They begin to tune their instruments. Listeners wait eagerly. A rich melody pours into the evening air. Then, above its steady beat, a solo begins to soar. The musician repeats the melody, then begins to change it and shape it in a distinctly different way. One by one, the players pass the melody and invent new ways for it to flow. This magical music is jazz. It has been flowing and changing for over a century. But its roots go back much further than that.

Jazz developed from music of the past. Enslaved Africans taken to the colonies in the 1700s brought the rhythms of their cultures with them. They developed work songs using these rhythms. Work songs used a pattern in which a leader called out a line and workers responded to the call. Spirituals let them pour their religious feelings and longing for freedom into song.

Songs such as these gave enslaved Africans ways of communicating. They showed the power of the human voice to express feelings. Their work songs and spirituals formed part of the foundation for jazz.

In the 1890s in New Orleans, a new form of music began. The blues combined instruments and powerful vocals. The songs expressed hardship and longing but also celebrated life. No matter how bad things got, the blues made people feel better.

New Orleans was a large city, a true melting pot. People from around the world brought their music with them. In New Orleans you could hear symphonies, church choirs, marching bands, and Latin dance bands. Ragtime pianists and blues musicians drew crowds. These different forms of music all played a part in the birth of jazz.

The Cotton Club, a music club in New York

Jazz music joined the feeling of blues with the off-beat tempo of ragtime. It was not predictable–it took the form of a song and let soloists play with it. The soloists' play was called improvisation. They made up music on the spur of the moment. Jazz musicians varied the tune to put their personal stamp on it.

Early in the twentieth century, many African Americans began moving north. Many wanted to leave impoverished lives in the South. They went to northern cities in search of better work. As they migrated, jazz and blues moved north with them.

World War I ended in 1918. The war's destruction left people sad. The horrors of war made many young people challenge old-fashioned ideas. The old ways had not protected the world from a terrible war. By the 1920s America was ready for the newness of jazz.

At the same time, America entered a prosperous era. The economy was booming. People had money to spend. They bought new inventions such as radios and record players. They listened joyfully to high-spirited jazz. It filled the airwaves and spread into homes and dance halls.

Duke Ellington and his band

Tough times returned in the 1930s. During the Great Depression, many people lost their jobs. People did not have money to spend on records or dance clubs. They had to worry about basics such as food and shelter. Many lost their homes, and some relied on soup kitchens for food. Nonetheless, many people had radios. Families gathered around the radio to listen to music. The soulful sounds of jazz spoke to them as never before.

As jazz grew more popular, large groups of jazz musicians began to play together. Out of these big bands, an exciting new style of jazz began. The big band sound, known as swing, swept the country.

In swing music, one section of the big band plays a rhythm pattern with a regular beat, while other individual players handle the rhythm differently. Swing took improvisation to a new level.

Lively swing music filled the airwaves. Its fast pace was great for dancing. The improvisation in music influenced dancing. It became freer, livelier, and more original. For those who had money, dance halls were the place to be. But those without much money loved swing too. It helped lift the spirits of a woeful nation. Big-band swing reminded Americans that the Depression would not last forever.

In the 1940s the United States was drawn into World War II. At home, materials such as plastic were hard to get. Few records were produced. Gas was rationed, so bands had trouble traveling from city to city.

African American jazz bands were not treated fairly. The war years were difficult years for them. Still, they continued to develop their art. New forms such as bebop appeared. Bebop included even more complex rhythms and tunes. Bebop solos contained more twists and turns than a mountain stream. Bebop was played at a very fast tempo.

More than a million African American soldiers served in the armed forces during the war. Many jazz musicians were among them. African American soldiers were separated from white troops. Often they were not treated with dignity. If they tried to eat or ride a bus with white soldiers, they could face abuse.

Many of the French treated them with a different attitude. African Americans abroad also saw that Europeans—especially the French—loved jazz! During the war jazz became a symbol of freedom in Paris. This respect influenced many African Americans. When they got home, many wanted more than ever to be treated as equals.

Louis Armstrong, a jazz musician, in Paris

Billie Holiday

The history of jazz is woven from a variety of colorful threads. Each new form of jazz has added to its richness. Many of the musicians who developed jazz are unknown. However, these giants of jazz are well loved.

Duke Ellington (1899–1974) was a pianist and bandleader. Ellington wrote over two thousand jazz songs and musicals. His music is still known and loved around the world.

Louis Armstrong (1901–1971) was born in New Orleans and grew up with jazz. He was known for his trumpet playing and scat singing. Scat involves singing nonsense syllables. It uses the voice like an instrument.

Billie Holiday (1915–1959) was a jazz singer. She was singing in clubs by the age of fifteen. Repeating the same songs bored her. She changed her voice and timing while singing the same words and melody.

Miles Davis (1926–1991) began his career playing bebop. Soon, however, he created his own style. He kept inventing new ways of making music. For example, he joined rock and pop music with jazz. Davis helped many other jazz artists get a start.

Many other talented people brought jazz to life.

During the 1950s Americans found new forms of entertainment. They began to watch television. Teenagers were caught up in rock-and-roll music. The jazz dance halls that were once crowded had to close their doors. However, talented new musicians took jazz in new directions.

Improvisation became freer. Smaller stage bands replaced the big bands of the past. Jazz solos grew longer. They also included more personal and imaginative twists. Even stronger changes of rhythm rose against the steady beat. Stage bands gave concerts. Record companies produced more jazz records. By the 1970s jazz had become popular once more!

True to its beginnings, jazz has continued to change over the years. It has been influenced by music from other cultures. It has also been adapted and used in other music forms. Rock-and-roll music has a steady beat. But some rock musicians grew bored with the repetition. They introduced jazz phrasing and solos over the steady beat.

Jazz was created by joining the best of many types of music. It continues to draw in elements of music from around the world. In turn, other cultures have borrowed from jazz to create new music. Jazz will continue to grow and change as new talent and ideas flow into the music.

Vocabulary

distinctly (di stingkt´ lē) (page 3) *adv.* Easily noticed or understood.

jazz (jaz) (page 3) *n.* Music that has strong rhythm and accented notes that fall in unexpected places.

blues (bl$\overline{oo}$z) (page 5) *n.* Music that sounds sad and has a jazz rhythm.

tempo (tem´ pō) (page 6) *n.* A rate of motion; pace.

predictable (pri dikt´ ə bəl) (page 6) *adj.* Expected; easily foretold.

impoverished (im pôv´ risht) (page 6) *adj.* Reduced to poverty; poverty-stricken.

prosperous (pros´ pər əs) (page 7) *adj.* Having success, wealth, or good fortune.

dignity (dig´ ni tē) (page 10) *n.* The condition of showing one's pride and worthiness in a confident manner.

Comprehension Focus: Adjusting Reading Speed

1. Read page 6. Then read it again slowly. How did adjusting your reading speed help you understand the information?
2. When did you find it necessary to adjust your reading speed? Why?